100 OF THE BEST CURSES + INSULTS IN SPANISH

To Margaret

Thank you Jeannine for great revisions and suggestions and irritating people the world over for inspiring the scenarios. Also special thanks to Eve Martinez, Antonio Martinez, Tesi Villanueva, Neil Dowden, and Silke Braun for all their work on the book.

Illustrations by Chuck Gonzales

Skyhorse Publishing books may be purchased in bulk at special discounts for sales promotion, corporate gifts, fund-raising, or educational purposes. Special editions can also be created to specifications. For details, contact the Special Sales Department, Skyhorse Publishing, 307 West 36th Street, 11th Floor, New York, NY 10018 or info@skyhorsepublishing.com.

Visit our website at www.skyhorsepublishing.com.

10 9 8 7 6 5 4 3 2 1

Library of Congress Cataloging-in-Publication data is available on file.

ISBN: 978-1616-08738-8

Printed and bound in China by South China Printing Co. Ltd

100 OF THE BEST CURSES + INSULTS IN SPANISH

by Rachel Perez with Antonio Martinez, illustrations by Chuck Gonzales

LEARN HOW TO GIVE 'EM HELL LIKE A NATIVE!

If you don't have anything nice to say, then say it! There are heaps of great put-downs, clever comebacks, unflattering analogies, and other unpleasantries to choose from, especially in Spanish! But wait a minute. With the beautiful beaches, great wine, enchanting music, laid-back companions, and all-night revelry, what could possibly go wrong? Well, you could be stomped on by a flamenco dancer, for one, bullied on the day of a bullfight, stabbed with toothpicks in a tapas frenzy, or even be mistaken for a piñata. What if some little rascals get their hands on your empanadas or your perfect view of *el mar* gets blocked by body parts that should never have seen the light of day?

When it comes to foul language, preoccupations with sex and genitalia cross cultural boundaries, as do garden-variety attacks on size and intelligence. Yet Spanish has quite a colorful array of ways to get even and come out on top. Sure, you should practice saying *buenos días, lo siento*, and *¿cómo están?*, but sometimes it's not a good day and you're not sorry. After all, a brutish woman could have cut you off on the sangria line after you waited an eternity for a taste of the fruity delight or a jackass with a mullet might be ruining every shot you take in Barcelona.

In this book, you'll find forty-five aggravating scenarios that you might—even in the land of *siestas* and *fiestas*—find yourself in, along with advice on how to get out of them, what to say, and why it's okay to say it.

Hopefully your trip will be as care- and incident-free as a walk in *el parque*. But if you find yourself hot under the collar in the land of the sun, you know where to turn. Whether you sling these, fling them, or pronounce them with delicacy and finesse, make sure you always get in the last word...or at least the most offensive.

PRONOUNCING SPANISH

Spelling and pronouncing Spanish are easy once you know the few basic rules. The chart below will help you with the pronunciation of the basic Spanish sounds and will give you a feeling for the rhythm of the language. The syllable to be stressed is marked in **bold** in the pronunciation.

SPANISH	SOUNDS LIKE	EXAMPLE	PRONUNCIATION
ca	ka	*cama*	**ka**-ma
co	ko	*con*	kon
cu	ku	*cubo*	**koo**bo
ce	the	*cena*	**the**-na
ci	thee	*cine*	**the** ene
ga	ga	*gato*	**ga**-to
go	go	*algo*	**al**go
gu	goo	*algún*	al**goon**
ge	khe	*gente*	**khen**te
gi	khee	*giro*	**khee**ro
j	kh	*jueves*	**khwe**-bes
ll	ly	*llamo*	**lya**-mo
ñ	ny	*señor*	se-**nyor**
ua	wa	*cual*	kwal
ue	we	*vuelva*	**bwel**ba
v	b	*vuelva*	bwelba
z	th	*Zaragoza*	tha-ra-**go**-tha

Here are a few more tips on Spanish pronunciation that will help you along the way:

• H is silent: *hora* is pronounced **o-ra**, and *hola* is pronounced **o-la**.
• R is rolled, and if you have rr, then the roll is more exaggerated.
• In Spanish, vowels (a, e, i, o, u) have only one sound. When you find two together, pronounce both of them in quick succession, as in *aceite*, **a-they-te**.

SITUATION #1: EMPANADA BANDIDOS

You duck into a cozy little café along an alleyway in Barrio Gótico, escaping the rain flooding the cobblestone streets and delighting in how family unfriendly the place looks. You ask for a glass of Abadia Retuerta and fantasize about all the ways you could spend this precious time alone. Should you attempt to read *Guía del Ocio*? Write your best friend a letter? Cast your eye around the room for an attractive stranger?

You almost sigh with delight as your waiter brings over the *tapas* you ordered, but just at that moment, a mom and five screaming kids plunk themselves down at the table next to you. Bad enough that they're ruining the ambiance, dropping peanuts like confetti, and blocking your view of any potentially attractive strangers, but one wily tween has the nerve to come over and pluck an empanada right off your plate.

What to do:

You could ask to move to another table or calmly tell the mother she needs to do a better job of controlling her hell *niños*, but really, this is between you, the pastry, and the prepubescent *bandido*. Think back to the playground days when some bully stole your Frisbee or ice cream cone. You know the rules about sticks and stones breaking bones, but words never hurting? Well, a few choice words in this situation will at least make YOU feel better, even if it leaves the *mocoso* (brat) scratching his head. The payoff will come later when he asks an adult what you meant.

What to say:

TIENES MÁS MORRO QUE UNA LATA DE CALLOS CADUCADA.

Literally: "You have got more snout than a tin of tripe past its sell-by date."

Basically: "You've got some nerve."

Why it's okay to say it:

The little thief will know you're mad, but he won't know exactly what you meant, which will make you a foreboding enough presence that he'll stay away from you and your lovely stuffed pastries for the rest of the evening.

In the know:

It's more socially acceptable to lightly discipline other people's offspring in Europe than it is in our "kids know best" environs where play dates and strollers reign. Back in the Old Country, the idea that children should be seen and not heard is still fairly in vogue, a convention that would surely please your grandmother. You're well within your rights to explain to the mother what happened, but let's face it — you'll have more fun stooping to the kid's level and hurling an insult or two his way. And you may need the practice: kids are perfectly welcome in bars in Spain.

EXTRA CREDIT

Picking on someone your own size is always a good idea, but sometimes you just can't resist. And why would you want to? Here are some schoolyard insults to keep in your back pocket:

TONTO meaning "dumb"

IDIOTA meaning "idiot"

IMBÉCIL meaning "moron"

SITUATION #2: REVENGE OF THE YANQUIS

You're having a great time at a Mediterranean restaurant in Valencia, except that you keep overhearing the wait staff loudly referring to you and your friends as *los yanquis*. True, you're downing Coca-Colas like you spent the day in the Sahara desert, and your brother-in-law's outfit screams Boston suburbia. Still, given how hard you've tried to blend in, you feel insulted by the undeserved pet name.

What to do:

Switch to English-only, talk about baseball and hot dogs, point to exotic dishes other people are eating and scrunch up your face in disgust, ask your waiter if they have any apple pie for dessert, and, on your way out, try to get a rousing version of the "Star Spangled Banner" going. (Be persistent; people may not join in at first, but never forget the famous Marseillaise scene in *Casablanca*.) Finally, just as you are about to slip out the door, double back, go over to your waiter, and let it rip.

What to say:

"ERES MÁS TONTO QUE MIS COJONES."

"You are stupider than my balls."

Though the literal translation in English lacks punch, this is a common insult in Spain, and its force will hit hard.

Why it's okay to say it:

You were polite customers and made every effort to follow the "when in Rome" tradition. By overdoing the *yanqui* act, then blindsiding the offender with a perfectly pronounced "in-the-know" put-down, you'll prove that this white boy knows how to salsa.

In the know:

The term *guiri* refers to a non-Spaniard (usually from America or Western Europe), but it is not necessarily a derisive term (think "gentile" for non-Jew).

EXTRA CREDIT

Here are some insults in several different languages spoken in Spain.

CASTILIAN (SPANISH): *CABRÓN*

This is literally a "billy goat", but when used as an insult it means "cuckold."

CATALAN: *FILL/FILLA DE PUTA*

"Son/daughter of a bitch"

GALICIAN: *COME BOSTAS*

"Eat shit"

EUSKERA: *ZOAZ PIKUTARA*

This is literally "Go to the shit"

SITUATION #3: CERVEZA GOGGLES

You're trying to scope out a tavern on your first night in Madrid when a guy with a run of pick-up lines more cringe-inducingly unoriginal than "Come here often?" (*¿Vienes aquí a menudo?*) won't get off your back. The tavern is hopping with sizzling Latino singles, and this cologne-ridden ne'er-do-well is giving everyone the impression that you two are an item by ordering drinks for you, sitting way too close, and pummeling you with these hideous lines whenever your attention wanders.

What to do:

First the hard part—refuse the next drink he buys. It may almost not seem worth it, but if you're going to break it off with someone who won't take a hint, you can't leave any room for uncertainty. Next time he orders you *una fría* (a cold beer), let him know it's a bridge to nowhere with a polite "*gracias pero no gracias.*" If he keeps touching your arm, tell him:

What to say:

VETE A TOMAR POR EL CULO, BABOSO.

"Go and take it up the ass, slime ball."

Baboso comes from *baba* ("drool"), and it's used for men who try to flirt with just about anyone in a disgusting, charmless way.

Why it's okay to say it:

It's only fair to let the guy know you're not interested. And with a few more drinks, you regrettably might be! Cut and run while the night is still young.

In the know:

Closing time in many cities in Spain puts "the city that never sleeps" to shame. It's true those Spaniards pack in a good afternoon siesta, but then they really live it up way past last call in New York. In Barcelona, it's common for nightclubs to stay open until 6 in the morning, and if you wait two hours, they'll open back up again for breakfast cocktails.

SITUATION #4: IS THAT A FERTILIZED EGG IN THERE OR ARE YOU JUST OVERWEIGHT?

Who can resist a hotel known as one of the most luxurious in Southern Spain? You should have known, though, that the staff of Hotel La Boladilla would be used to beautiful people with figures a little more svelte than yours. Still, the hostess who rubbed your belly and said "*Felicidades*" ("Congratulations") was way too forward, not to mention the fact that, unless something went horribly wrong the night before, you're not expecting.

What to do:
Smile politely, order a whisky from the bar, take a giant swig, rub the hostess' belly and ask her:

What to say:
¿SABE USTED SI ES UN NIÑO O UNA NIÑA?

"Do you know if it's a boy or a girl?"

Or, if you're really infuriated and want to abandon the art of subtlety, then say:

ESTÁ TAN GORDA QUE SU ULTIMO PEDO SE MIDIÓ EN LA ESCALA DE RICHTER.

"You are so fat that your last fart was measured on the Richter scale."

Why it's okay to say it:

It's never forgivable to assume someone
is with child. Sure, you may be a bit out of shape, and
you've probably done a little too much snacking and not
enough walking on those evening tapas bar strolls (*ir de
tapeo*) but, until you see someone grunting in stirrups,
you never assume she's pregnant. This *señora* was either
hinting that your *vestido* was getting a little too tight, or
simply being presumptuous and insensitive.

In the know:

Latin cultures tend to be a lot more direct about com-
menting on physical appearance in a not-so-flattering
way. It's not unusual to hear people affectionately
refer to an overweight friend as *gordo or gordito* (fat),
a short friend as *enano or enana* (dwarf), or someone
with a prominent nose as *narigudo/nariguda or napión*
(big-nosed).

EXTRA CREDIT

To avoid the common mistake of trying to say that you're embarrassed and acciden-
tally announcing an immaculate conception, here are some vulgar slang terms for
when you do see a little pink dot:

PREÑADA or **ESTAR CON BOMBO**

"*Bombo*" is a bass drum, so this is literally telling someone they have a "drum for
a belly."

SITUATION #5: BATTLE OF THE BULGE

Ah, the Costa del Sol—the sun, the olive trees, the ocean breeze, the...unsightly bulges! With free public beaches in Marbella you expected a crowd, and you'd been warned about small-time thieves, but this Speedo fashion crime is more than you can tolerate even on a good day.

What to do:

Put on your sunglasses, shield your eyes, and face your towel the other way. If there's another clear space, it's worth your while to move...especially since the last thing you want to do is flatter the intruders in an otherwise flawless landscape. Be careful not to give any attention to the men in their "barely there" swimsuits. Before you duck and run, however, turn to the exhibitionist offenders and say:

What to say:

ERES MÁS FEO QUE ENVIAR A TU ABUELA A POR DROGA.

"You are uglier than sending your granny to buy you some drugs."

Why it's okay to say it:

There's a story behind the name Marbella. On a trip to the coast, Queen Isabelle is said to have remarked on the beautiful scene: "¡Qué mar tan bello!" ("What a beautiful ocean!"). It's your right to enjoy it as well; if you'd wanted to squint at bizarre and unbalanced proportions, you'd have spent the day at the Picasso museum.

In the know:

A few days into your jaunt along coastal Spain and chances are you'll welcome the sight of *any* suit at all, after seeing the number of birthday suits out and about. Most beaches in Spain are clothing optional, and Europeans famously let it all hang out on holiday. If you're up for an extreme au natural experience, there are naturist beaches and nudist colonies aplenty; just be sure you're clear about where you can and can't plant your bare *nalgamen* (bottom, ass).

SITUATION #6: THE SUN ALSO PRESSES THE SNOOZE BUTTON

You've dreamed of Sevilla ever since the first time you heard "Toreador's Song" from *Carmen*. You decide this is the one city where you're going to forget about blending in and embrace your role as a visitor, so you sign up for a tour starting from Casa de Pilatos. It's a blistering hot day and there's little shade to be found as more and more people join you, with no sign of the tour guide. In the end, you wait a full hour before *el guía* (the guide) strolls up nonchalantly, waving an Andalusian fan, and saying "Welcome to Sevilla, *¿cómo están?*" ("how are you?")

What to do:
Pointing to your watch and asking if the *bobo* (dummy) knows what time it is will get you nowhere. He'll likely respond that you need to relax and enjoy; he's just trying to help you get acclimated to the culture. Instead, tell him you write for several travel magazines and you were hoping to put in a good word for his services. You're sure to get the royal treatment, and maybe even a few freebies. But if the scorching Spanish sun has driven you mad with rage, then it's time to take action.

What to say:
SI NO ME DEVUELVES EL DINERO TE CORTO LOS COJONES
"Either you give me my money back, or I will slice your balls."

Why it's okay to say it:

True, the Spanish tend to be more laid back than us, and late arrivals can be a source of pride, but this little *gilipollas* (pr**ck) is just hiding behind the culture differences as an excuse. He knows travelers have itineraries to follow, and he owes you big time for messing up yours. You have a right to be annoyed by the aggressive tardiness, but do try to enjoy the slower pace of Southern Spain or you may miss out on all that it has to offer.

In the know:

If the late arrival thing starts to bug you, take comfort in the fact that Spain isn't even the worst offender. In Argentina, it's actually considered rude to show up on time.

EXTRA CREDIT

Seville's motto is sometimes taken to mean "It [Seville] has not abandoned me." That's all very well and good, but there may be times you want to tell your Sevillian friends to get lost. If so, try the following:

VETE A HACER PUÑETAS

VETE A HACER GÁRGARAS

Both of these common expressions could be translated as "go to hell," but the first one literally means "go and do some complicated embroidery on cuffs," and the second literally translates to "go and gargle." They aren't terribly offensive, so feel free to use them with friends and family.

SITUATION #7: TWO LEFT FEET

Dance isn't really your thing, but of course you can't leave Andalucía without witnessing the exotic spectacle of flamenco dance. You're entranced by the colorful costumes, the energetic clapping and sound of the castanets, the seductive music, and the fanciful steps of the performers. Then, suddenly, out of nowhere, one twirling dervish stomps hard on your foot before turning and smiling an almost demonic grin.

What to do:

Join the dance. Don't worry about the steps; just throw yourself into the chaos of it until you get close enough to your opponent to stomp on her foot and say:

What to say:

TIENES MENOS GRACIA QUE KUNG FU
BAILANDO SEVILLANAS.

"You are as graceful as a Kung-fu dancing flamenco."

Tener gracia means to be graceful, to have a flair for something, so this is a sarcastic expression intended to insult.

Why it's okay to say it:

She should have at least given you a "*Disculpa*" (mistake) if it were truly an accident. And unfortunately for you, unlike most dancers, flamenco dancers aren't exactly light on their feet.

In the know:

Although there are different theories about its exact origins, flamenco is associated with gypsy culture and has ties to India and the Middle East. We often think of the dancers when we hear the word "flamenco," but it's the *cante* (singing) that's actually at the center of the tradition. Originally it was accompanied by *palmas* (hand clapping) with the guitar added to the mix in the 19th century.

EXTRA CREDIT

In English we say someone has "two left feet" when they're clumsy. Here are some equivalent terms in Spanish:

TORPE (clumsy)

PATOSO

Pataso comes from *pato* which means "duck," so this could be translated to mean walking or behaving like a duck.

SITUATION #8: URBAN SOMBRERO

For most of your time in the Basque country, you've been attempting to soak up the culture, but one afternoon you sneakily duck into a movie theater to see the latest James Bond flick. The place is packed, but luckily the guy in front of you is on the small side. As soon as he takes off his sombrero, you'll be fine...only the previews are over, the credits are starting, and that damn sombrero's got more staying power than General Franco.

What to do:

Lean your head to his side and rest it right next to his shoulder. When he gives you an annoyed look, explain that you can't see past his shade-maker. If he still doesn't take it off, let him know you're not down with the whole Speedy González act by quietly whispering the following...

What to say:

ME CAGO EN EL COPÓN, QUÍTATE EL SOMBRERO O TE LO QUITO A HOSTIAS.

The insult here comes from the use of the religious objects — "chalice" (*copón*) and "host" (*hostia*) — in a vulgar way. Some of the worst insults and vulgar expressions in Spanish have religious implications.

In the know:

Many cities have *el día de espectador*—a 50% discount to the movies, often on Wednesdays. American films are usually dubbed, but if the Milli Vanilli lips bother you, or you won't understand the Spanish, opt for subtitles by finding *versión original subtitulada*.

EXTRA CREDIT

Maybe it's all the *fútbol* (soccer) or mad rushes for sangría, but Spanish has quite a few ways to say "obstacle." Here are a few of them:

IMPEDIMENTO, BACHE, ESTORBO, TRABA.

SITUATION #9: ASHES TO ASSES

You're having a great time barhopping in Valencia. It's warm out, so you don't have to put your jacket on and off, the bartenders let you take your wine outside, smoke inside, and basically live it up. Too bad the night takes a turn for the worse when this *borracho* (drunk man) who has been burping and spilling beer on you all night flicks his cigarette ashes on your lap. You don't want to be labeled an "ugly American," but this guy violates enough etiquette to give Emily Post a second career.

What to do:

Light a match, put it under your face (think Jack Nicholson in *The Shining*) and tell him...

What to say:

VETE A DORMIR LA MONA O TE QUEMO LOS HUEVOS.

"Go to sleep it off or I'll burn your balls."

The literal translation means "Go and sleep the female monkey," since *mona* means "monkey," but it is also a slang word for drunkenness.

Why it's okay to say it:

There's no excuse for this kind of carelessness, and even if the bozo apologizes, the damage is done. You're well within your rights to scare the guy and let him know you'll be watching him the rest of the night.

In the know:

Americans are often surprised at the number of people who still smoke in Spain. In 2006, the smoking ban went into effect for all public places in Spain, but restaurants and bars can choose whether or not they allow it.

EXTRA CREDIT

You can call someone who has had a few too many drinks a *borracho*, but it's fun to pull out more colorful terms. Here are a couple ways to say "shit-faced" in Español:

IR TAJADO

ESTAR COMO UNA CUBA "literally, to be like a barrel/cask"

PILLAR UNA JUMERA

SITUATION #10: RUNNING OF THE BULLIES

July in Pamplona means only one thing: la Fiesta de Los Sanfemines and the celebrated running of the bulls. You decide to join in the 900-yard dash; after all, what are the chances you'll be one of the hundreds of people injured every year?

You know full well the risk of injury but, with all that merriment, you hadn't given any thought to risk of insult. As you plug along on Santo Domingo, cursing your lapsed gym member-ship and all those frothy Starbucks Frappucinnos, you overhear a group of snarky twenty-somethings laughing at you. You let it slide until one of them calls out, "Are you moving forward or backward?"

What to do:

You could turn both cheeks by moon-ing the hecklers as you sprint past, or you could think faster than you run and hurl this doozy their way...

What to say:

METEROS UN PALO POR EL CULO, COMEMIERDAS.

Literally: "Stick a stick up your ass, shit eaters."

Basically: "F**ck off."

Why it's okay to say it:

You were just trying to get into the spirit of things and figured as long as you stayed in front of the bulls, you were doing all right. Besides, who are they to make fun of you if they don't even have the guts to join in?

In the know:

Before the *encierro* (running of the bulls), it is tradition for runners to sing:

> *A San Fermín pedimos, por ser nuestro patrón, nos guíe en el encierro dándonos su bendición.*

> "To San Fermin we ask, because he is our patron, to guide us in the run and give us his blessing."

Most people receive it, but on average two to three hundred people are still injured each year.

EXTRA CREDIT

"Cheeks" is a relatively pleasant way to refer to the backside. What are some affectionate terms for "tush" in Spanish?

PANDERO, TRASERO, POMPIS

SITUATION #11: FÚTBOL FOLLIES

It's Sunday night and you're doing your best to mingle at an after-*fútbol* match party in Vigo, but just as you move from one group of acquaintances to another, you hear the first group quickly talk about going somewhere else. You wouldn't be surprised if they left without telling you, but you are a bit offended to hear they're scheming about how to get your tall, dark, and handsome friend to *apuntarse* (accompany them) but ditch you. The final insult is hearing them call you *soso* (boring), especially after you spent the whole night rooting for Celta de Vigo when you couldn't have given a rat's ass who won.

What to do:

Try a few fancy drilling moves to hit the ankles of these *hinchas* (soccer fans). When they look up, just explain that you were inspired by tonight's fancy footwork. Then find your friend and blow that joint. The *gillipollas* (pr**cks) can't ditch you if you're already gone. On your way out of the party (arm in arm with your friend of course), glance back once at the offender who called you "boring" and sweetly say...

What to say:

SOIS MÁS DESAGRADABLES QUE LA NIÑA DEL EXORCISTA

Literally: "You are more unpleasant than the girl in *The Exorcist*."

Why it's okay to say it:

These *idiotas* were acting like they were in a sit-com, talking at full volume a few feet away from you as if you wouldn't overhear.

In the know:

Soccer (*fútbol*) is by far Spain's most popular national sport, often compared to a religion because of its massive and devout following. Despite top rankings in FIFA (Fédération Internationale de Football Association), Spain has never won the World Cup.

EXTRA CREDIT

Food often comes in handy as a way to describe someone's personality (see Situation #45). In English, we call someone "vanilla" to mean they're plain and unoriginal, and Seinfeld popularized the term "vegetable lasagna" to describe a dull person. How do the Spanish get across that someone is perfectly pleasant but doesn't add anything to the punch bowl?

SOSO, SOSAINA, SOSERAS, OR *DESABORÍO*

SITUATION #12: ANCIENT TRUTHS

You're the oldest member of a group at a tour of the Old Masters in Madrid's Museo del Prado. You're starting to resent how the 80-year-old curator keeps looking at you and saying "*¿Verdad?*" when talking about the way things used to be. This ancient wonder has at least two decades on you, and you're pretty sure when people call Spain "the country of the sun," they're picturing his face. Why would he even think to class you as "age buddies?"

What to do:
This is a great chance to employ the old adage "don't get mad, get even." Wait until you get to the collection of chiaroscuro. Stop in front of one of Jose de Ribera's masterpieces of St. Jerome looking wan, wrinkled, and decrepit. Turn to the guide and say:

What to say:

¡NO SABÍA QUE SE SACARA UN SOBRESUELDO HACIENDO DE MODELO!

"I didn't know you got some extra cash by modeling!"

Why it's okay to say it:
This guy asked for it. Instead of applauding you for keeping up with a group of people half your age, he's poking at you, hoping to get a rise. Your patience and calculated revenge will show him you're a faster moving target than he had pegged you for.

In the know:

Be careful when talking, or especially writing, about "years" in Spanish. *Año* is "year"; but without the tilde above the "n," it actually means "anus."

SITUATION #13: THE RAIN IN SPAIN

You came prepared for the rain in Galicia, tucking your adorable little green umbrella into your purse so you'll have it at the ready. One morning, the sky opens up suddenly just as you step out of El Castillo. You pop it open and you're dry and comfy, strolling down the hill while people all around you are running for cover. Unfortunately, one (not particularly handsome) stranger decides to take shelter under your umbrella. At first you think it's just a coincidence that he's so close, but you speed up, slow down, do a head fake left, then turn right; no matter what, he stays right with you.

What to do:

You could bite your nose to spite your face and close up your umbrella, or duck into a store with the other rain-soaked travelers, but why should you? After all, you remembered your umbrella! No matter what you decide, make sure that you at least give this guy a piece of your mind first...

What to say:

TIENES MÁS CARA QUE UN SACO DE SELLOS/ MONEDAS

Literally: "You've got more face than a sack full of stamps/coins."

Basically: "You are shameless, you've got some nerve."

In Spanish, *tener cara* ("to have face") means to have nerve, and because stamps and coins tend to show faces, this is how the insult was derived.

Why it's okay to say it:

Girl Scout that you are, you came prepared and the umbrella wasn't meant for two. The very least he owes you is a "Don't mind if I do?" to which you would have clearly responded that you do in fact mind. Teach him not to cut in, but be prepared to weather some insults yourself.

SITUATION #14: : IN VINO VERITAS

You're on a tour of a family-run winery that boasts a fantastic array of sparkling wines. All is going well except the owner has absolutely no sense of personal space. Every time he pours you a cup of Gloria Ferrer or Carta Nevada Brut, he stands right next to you, practically keeping his hand on yours and watching your lips as you taste it. Plus, he seems to need an absolutely ridiculous amount of feedback from you, and you're tired of smiling and saying "*delicioso*" every few minutes.

What to do:

Stop backing away; you're creating a feedback cycle where you step back, he steps forward, and the tango continues. Instead, follow so close on his heels that you step on them, peer right into his face at every turn, and for God's sake, stop praising the booze. Hopefully he'll back off. And if he doesn't...

What to say:

ERES MÁS PESADO QUE UNA VACA EN BRAZOS

Literally: "You are heavier than carrying a cow."

Basically: "You are a pain in the neck."

Pesado means both "pain in the neck" and "heavy".

Why it's appropriate:

You signed up for a tour of the winery, not his anatomy. To be honest, you don't think he's interested in you (although he did wink when he referenced shipping wine in bulk to supply Roman orgies). Still, he needs to shut up about letting the wine breathe and give *you* a little breathing room!

In the know:

Spain is known for great and affordable wines, sparkling varieties, and sherries (including the world famous Tío Pepe), and the tradition of making wine goes back to Phoenician times. Who knows? Maybe all the great and affordable hooch explains why the Spanish have such a different understanding of personal space than we do.

EXTRA CREDIT

If you did want to insult the wine, how do you say it's disgusting? Here, gag me with a *cuchara* (spoon):

ASQUEROSO, VOMITIVO,* and *INFECTO

all mean "disgusting." And if the wine tastes like "shit," then why beat around the bush?

UNA MIERDA

SITUATION #15: VISTA CONQUISTADOR

You're trying to pack in the sights in Barcelona with your tour group, but this *idiota* sporting a mullet is blocking every photo op. He obstructs your view of the bell towers at the Catedral de Barcelona, jumps in at the last second as you snap the Columbus monument on the waterfront at sundown, cuts a diagonal right across the fountains at Montjuic, and rears his ugly head in all three panoramic shots you take from Tibidabo. If it were any other city you might not mind, but your late father was killed after a freak accident in the Big Cats exhibit at the Barcelona Zoo, and it really meant a lot to you to capture the essence of the place he spent his final days.

What to do:
At first you thought he was just bullying his way in front of you, but then you start to realize this Rod Stewart look-alike is actually intent on making cameos in your shots. You may need to pull an *Iñigo Montoya* on him.

What to say:

ERES MÁS PESADO QUE UN COLLAR DE MELONES!

Literally: "You are heavier than a necklace made out of melons!"

Basically: "You are being a pain in the ass!"

Pesado means "heavy" and "a pain."

Why it's okay to say it:

This is more than just travel photography; this is an homage to your family history. A buzz cut or even a Mohawk could have been overlooked, but this *greñas* (person with a mullet) is just unforgivable.

In the know:

Unfortunately, the mullet is enjoying a renaissance in Spain and is now seen as "vintage retro." The Spanish mullet tends to be shorter than our version, thankfully stopping at the top of the shoulders.

SITUATION #16: DROPPING THE EAVESDROPPER!

After three weeks in the Sierra Nevada cut off from the web, you decide to connect to the "real" world. Inside an internet café in the Costa Blanca, you set yourself up with a *café solo* and launch Internet Explorer. You see thirty new messages in your inbox and wonder if there are any of interest. After a quick scan, you're thrilled to discover one from your minor office crush. You're relishing every word when you feel the eyes of a stranger. And what's even worse is that they're not on you, but on your computer screen!

What to do:

Open a new message and write in an aggressively large font, "You'll never believe how obnoxious some Spaniards can be. I am in a café and this *mujer* is watching my screen like it's a *telenovela* (soap opera)."

If she ignores your obvious annoyance and the ogling continues, then it's up to you to re-direct her attention.

What to say:

¿YA LOS VES BIEN O PREFIERES QUE TE LOS EMPOTRE EN TU PUTA CARA?

"Can you see them properly or shall I smack them on your f**cking face?"

Why it's okay to say it:

Unlike many activities in España, email is NOT a spectator sport.

In the know:

Internet cafes are an easy find in Spain and throughout Europe. Equipped for people traveling on business or pleasure, they usually have printers, photocopiers, and faxes available. For more fun, visit a *churrería* café where you can partake in a national favorite: *churros y chocolate*.

EXTRA CREDIT

Words you'd love to call your crush but would never put in an email:

TÍO/TÍA BUENA

A gorgeous guy/girl

ESTAR COMO UN QUESO

Literally: to be (as nice as) cheese

ESTAR FOLLABLE

Literally: To be f**ckable

SITUATION #17: NOT SO JOLLY GIANT

You're in the Guggenheim museum in Bilbao enjoying Richard Serra's sculptures in the Arcelor Gallery. You've already spent half the morning just admiring the exterior design, so you're trying to be expedient getting through the permanent collection. There's just one problem. Every few minutes a giant pseudo-artist type carrying a sketchpad bumps straight into you and doesn't even bother to say "*perdón*" (excuse me). Sure, you might be a bit vertically challenged, but what are you supposed to do, hold up a traffic cone?

What to do:

Next time Supersize-Me smacks into you, hit him where it hurts and pretend it's an accident. Given that your shoulders come up roughly to his crotch, he's in dangerous territory. As far as what to say, you're probably best served by a saccharine smile and telling him:

What to say:

APARTA COLEGA QUE ERES MÁS LARGO QUE UN DÍA SIN PAN.

"Move out of the way my friend, you are longer than a day without bread."

The word *colega* is a slang word for "friend."

Why it's okay to say it:

An art exhibit should be a peaceful experience; it's true you're supposed to gain a new way of seeing the world, but "How's the weather up there?" homey needs to work on the *old* way of seeing it too.

EXTRA CREDIT

Insulting someone's physical appearance might be a low blow, but a true artist will utilize all mediums. Here are some Spanish insults about size and shape:

ENANO ("dwarf")

MESA CAMILLA (this is a small round table covered with a long cloth, and it's used to play cards, have coffee, etc. Calling someone a *mesa camilla* implies they're "fat").

FOCA ("SEAL" means fat)

TONEL ("BARREL" means fat)

FIDEO ("noodle" means thin)

MÁS LARGO QUE UN DÍA SIN PAN

(literally translates to "longer than a day without bread," and is meant to insult tall people)

SITUATION #18: THOU SHALL NOT MOOCH

You're enjoying the balmy night air in Granada and a casual *botellón* (an informal and social street gathering). You and your friends are well-stocked with cheap but delicious table wines from the neighborhood *mercado* (market), but the group next to you is not quite as prepared. They're friendly and introduced themselves to you right away. (You did briefly wonder if they were kidding with their names—Jesús, Angel, Jose María, and María Jose—but no one else laughed.) It was fine to give them a round or two, but the night has just begun, and they've already hit you up more times than the tithe collectors at Our Lady of Mercy. They may think water turns into wine, but your *vino* (wine) is the old-fashioned kind, picked from the vine, stomped on, and paid for with hard-earned *dinero* (money).

What to do:
Tell these pilgrims that that the "feeding the multitudes" portion of the evening is over, and they'll have to look elsewhere. If they still don't lay off, tell them:

What to say:

TIENES MÁS CARA QUE ESPALDA

Literally: "Your face is bigger than your back."

Basically: "You've got some nerve!"

Cara literally means "face," but it can also mean "nerve."

Why it's okay to say it:

Buying rounds for friends is perfectly acceptable in Spain, and most will return the favor. Local wines are often cheaper than buying soda or bottled water, so this group's steadfast refusal to buy a bottle of their own is only making you look like a *primo* (sucker).

In the know:

Americans will be delighted to discover that drinking outdoors is perfectly legal in Spain (no brown bag needed!), and you can also buy wine, beer, and alcohol at any supermarket. You should know, however, that large gatherings like *botellones* are banned in certain Spanish cities, including Madrid. Nationally, the drinking age is 18, but it's not enforced.

EXTRA CREDIT

Here are some informal ways to say "freeloader" in Spanish:
GORRÓN, JETAS, AGARRAO,* OR *CHUPÓN.

SITUATION #19: AIRCRAFT GUITAR

You finally ditched your almost-in-laws after a solid week of listening to Larry practice rolling his *r*'s and Helen acting surprised at the people drinking *Calimochos* (a mix of Coke and wine). You and your fiancé are alone and looking forward to a night on the town in Salamanca. You choose *Chez Víctor*, reportedly the city's best restaurant. You're just picking out a wine and skimming the surface of all the venting you want to do when a *guitarrista* (guitarist) catches your eye and sidles over to your table. You instantly engage your fiancé, silently cursing yourself for the accidental eye contact. The *guitarrista* doesn't take your hint and launches into a seemingly unending catalog of romantic serenades.

What to do:

Try to let your body language do the talking here. Don't smile, don't nod appreciatively, and avoid looking in his general direction at all. If that doesn't work, try talking loudly over the music. If he hasn't stopped when the *frutas* and *café* arrive, then it's time to take immediate action.

What to say:

VETE A FREIR ESPARRAGOS

Literally: "Go and fry some asparagus!"

Basically: "Get lost!"

Why it's okay to say it:

You feel a little sorry for the guy; he's getting pushed around like a hot potato, but he is being inconsiderate, ruining your one moment of peace by hovering around like an alien spacecraft.

In the know:

Beer with lemonade or lemon Fanta? Wine with coke or orange soda? While these concoctions conjure up the image of college students trying to stretch minimum wage earnings as far as possible on a Saturday night, you'll see them all over bars and restaurants in Spain. Andalusians are particularly proud of their *tinto de verano* (wine served on ice mixed with lemonade). Whoever thought wine coolers could be so classy?

EXTRA CREDIT

If you ever do get a moment alone, what will you do with your fiancé? How do you say "let's get it on" in the language of love?

FOLLAR

MOJAR

ECHAR UN POLVO

Only use the suggestions above if you're trying to be direct, since these literally translate to "to f**ck."

SITUATION #20: SANGRÍA WARS

You've waited so long in the sangría line at the fiesta in the Barrio Santa Cruz that you're wondering if that lovely red, splashing liquid is a mirage. You're definitely starting to confuse the *jarras* (pitchers) with the painting of the Holy Grail you saw earlier that day at the Cathedral of Seville. You're just about at the front of the line when a brawny woman muscles ahead of you, proving that Spanish bravado is indeed alive and well.

What to do:

Summon your inner *torero* (bullfighter) and fight to the finish. Nothing comes between you and your fruity spirits!

What to say:

ERES UN CACHO CARNE CON OJOS.

Literally: "You are a piece of meat with eyes."
Basically: "You are stupid, brute, and simple."

Why it's okay to say it:

You may not be a wine aficionado and you've never figured out if legs are good or bad, but you'll go one-on-one any day with someone who wants to talk chopped lemons, oranges, and enough sugar to send all of Puerta del Sol into diabetic shock.

In the know:

Sangría is a party drink in Spain. For the most part, only *touristas* order it in a bar. If you don't mind being spotted as one, then bottoms up; do know, however, that bartenders tend to jack up prices for *yanquis* (Americans).

EXTRA CREDIT

Except for the drink shortage, the party is a lot of fun. What do you call a party that's a total bust?

UN ROLLO

UN COÑAZO

SITUATION #21: SOMEONE IN PORTUGAL CAN'T HEAR YOU

You're enjoying the peace and solitude inside a monastery in Burgos when out of nowhere a tall, thin, obnoxiously good-looking woman sits next to you in the cloisters, talking sales figures and business plans into her cell phone. It's obviously unacceptable to be talking on a phone in church, but what really *te molesta* (annoys you) is that this is the *worst* form of shrill cell phone chatter. Even gossip or relationship babbling would be easier to swallow.

What to do:

If you can't beat 'em, join 'em! When someone won't let you ignore them, then don't! Let her know you're listening. Nod when she nods, exclaim "Wow!" and "Uh huh," or interject a "Hmm, not sure if I agree" while she's chittering away. Hopefully you'll annoy her a little, and if you're lucky, unnerve her a lot.

What to say:

¿NO ME DIGAS?

Do you think so?

¿DE VERDAD?

Really?

¡VAYA!

What?!

Why it's okay to say it:

There should be a name to describe people like this, the ones who confuse talking on the phone in a flamboyant manner, constantly checking their BlackBerries, and updating their Facebook status ("networking") with work. At dinner parties and family get-togethers, they get continual credit for being such "work animals"; meanwhile, they have the attention span of a fruit fly. You're doing the world a service by giving this one a good swat.

In the know:

Texting is extremely popular in Spain, even more so than in the U.S. They even have a fixation with something called *toque* where you let someone know you got a message by "tapping" them via phone. It could save a lot of anguish wondering whether or not you're phone stalking someone or if they're simply not getting your messages!

EXTRA CREDIT

Sometimes you want to say goodbye and good riddance. Here are some Spanishisms for signing off when you're annoyed:

¡QUÉ TE DEN MORCILLAS!

Literally: "I hope they give you some black pudding!"

¡QUÉ TE DEN POR EL CULO!

"I hope you get buggered!"

SITUATION #22: PLANETA OF THE APES

You're listening to a talk on evolution at the National Museum of Natural History and, outside of a few blank faces, most people are really enjoying it. One guy up front, however, keeps laughing the most obnoxious, fake, forced laugh whenever the speaker pauses. This guy is making a better case for evolution than the Ph.D. on stage!

What to do:

Take notes to help you focus on the lecture and try to ignore the jungle sound effects. Depending on how intrusive the heckling is, decide whether or not to drop your bomb during or after the lecture. If possible, address him afterward. If he's visibly rattling the speaker and making concentration for everyone difficult, then it's time to put this *mono* (ape) in the limelight.

What to say:

¿TE HAS ESCAPADO DEL ZOO?

"Have you run away from the zoo?"

Why it's okay to say it:

You tried to wait until after the lecture so you could catch the offender in private, and you probably wouldn't have said anything at all if he'd had the decency to laugh at the speaker's jokes as well.

In the know:

Almost 75% of Spaniards believe in evolution and another 5% are not sure. Compare that to the U.S. where only about 42% believe, and that should put the heckling into perspective.

EXTRA CREDIT

Ever wonder if other countries use Neanderthal or caveman as insults? Here are the Spanish versions:

HOMBRE DE LAS CAVERNAS (literally "caveman")

CROMAÑON

TROGLODITA

SITUATION #23: "ARE WE HAVING FUN YET?"

Your friends Bill and Katy are visiting you from the States and you've been doing back flips all weekend to entertain them. You took them out to dinner at El Viajero, treated them to the opera, and took cabs to as many sights as possible. The problem is they won't tell you what they want to do, they are wholly unimpressed with every sight, and nothing you suggest seems to interest them. Their lackluster responses are driving you insane: "You know us, we don't care," *Ni fú ni fá* ("Neither good nor bad") or "Whatever *you* feel like doing." Well, what you feel like doing is going back in time and not having them visit!

What to do:
Stop jumping through hoops, first of all. It's not having any effect. There will always be times when friends and family annoy you to the point of explosion, and you'll need to unleash some personal vitriol. Next time they give a dreary, indifferent response to a suggestion you make, say:

What to say:

SOIS MÁS SOSOS QUE UN YOGUR DE AGUA

Literally: "You are duller than a water-flavored yogurt."

Why it's okay to say it:

You're giving them the royal treatment, and they can't even show a little enthusiasm. It's just plain rude, and your fear of awkwardness shouldn't come in the way of making it clear that you're annoyed.

In the know:

Most Madrileños do speak some English, so if you do need to let your friends loose on the city, they'll likely be fine doing "whatever" on their own.

EXTRA CREDIT

If you want to express frustration in Spanish, try this one on for size:

ME CAGO EN LA LECHE

"I shit in the milk."

HOSTIA PUTA

This is a combination of "host" (religious sense) and "whore." It's used as an expression of frustration, closest in English to saying "F**ck!" or "Bloody hell!"

LA MADRE QUE ME PARIÓ

"The mother who gave birth." Just like hostia puta, this is just a term used to express frustration like exclaiming "Shit!" or "F**ck!"

SITUATION #24: SIESTAS FOR THE REST OF US

You've always been a bit of a cat-napper, so you were thrilled to take advantage of Spain's wonderful siesta tradition. After the fireworks at the Festival de la Cereza in Alfarnate, plus *las palmas* (the flamenco session) all last night, you were really looking forward to a few hours of shut-eye this afternoon. Unfortunately, the honeymoon couple in the next room doesn't seem to know the meaning of the word "siesta," and their interpretation of a cherry festival seems to involve popping more than just champagne bottles.

What to do:

There's not much you can do here, other than the old-fashioned bang on the wall and admonishment that "Some of us are trying to get some sleep around here!" It's not likely to have much of an impact, unless you can time it exactly right.

What to say:

¡PODÉIS ACABAR DE UNA PUTA VEZ? SOIS MÁS LENTOS QUE UNA PROCESIÓN DE BERBERECHOS!

"Hurry the f**ck up, you are slower than a procession of cockles!"

Why it's okay to say it:

Sleeping in the afternoon is a national right. 'Nuff Enough. (Ya!)

In the know:

The tradition of the siesta is often attributed to the scorching temperatures in many parts of Spain as well as the large middle-of-the-day meal. It is believed that people working in the fields would traditionally take a break during the hottest part of the day (mid-afternoon) and return to work through the evening. The long lunch and period of rest goes hand-in-hand with the late nights. It's not unusual for people of all ages to routinely stay out until 3 in the morning. In the past, stores and businesses would close during the extended lunch, but the practice is gradually disappearing from big city life, where the strains of the 24–7 global economy have made their mark.

EXTRA CREDIT

Swear words are taken from body parts in many languages, and Spanish is no exception:

COJONES ("balls")

COÑO ("c**nt")

HERRAMIENTA (a euphemism for "penis"; literally: "tool")

HIGO (This translates to "vagina," and is considered vulgar)

SITUATION #25: LOGORRHEA

You decide to bring your new boyfriend, Esteban, to a family dinner at El Portico forgetting that when he's nervous, his mouth drips bathroom humor faster than a leaky faucet. As soon as the waiter wishes you *"Buen provecho"* ("Enjoy your meal"), the obscene jokes start pouring out. You do everything you can to put a lid on it, but when Esteban compares the rounded barstools at the restaurant to a woman's breasts, your mother finally gets up and leaves the table.

What to do:

If verbal Imodium existed, you'd give him a triple dose, but there's not much you can do here other than dominate the conversation as much as possible. When you get a moment alone with him, say:

What to say:

ERES MÁS BASTO QUE UNAS BRAGAS DE ESPARTO.

"You are coarser than underwear made of sparto grass fabric."

Sparto grass fabric is a rough material used to make sandals and the heels of mules. With this insult, you'd pretty much be telling someone that they're coarser than underwear made of wicker!

Why it's okay to say it:

A vulgar sense of humor (*sentido de humor ordinario*) is one thing, but your sidekick's conversation is really *de mal gusto* (in poor taste).

In the know:

Wildly inappropriate stuff aside, the Spanish are somewhat old-fashioned when it comes to table manners. You can't put your elbows on the table, but you can't put them on your lap either. Instead, keep your hands on the table, next to the plate. Keep the conversation flowing in a good way, as the Spanish aren't used to silence at the table. In fact it's so rare, they have a poetic way to describe it: "*Ha pasado un angel*" ("An angel passed over").

EXTRA CREDIT

With varying degrees of intensity from least offensive to positively sickening, here's how to say vulgar in Spanish:

GROSERO

"Crude"

ASQUEROSO

"Repugnant"

VOMITIVO

"Sickening"

SITUATION #26: DON JUAN WANNABE

You're on a date with a guy who'd been asking you out for weeks. You finally said yes just to get him to stop, and during the entire date he brings up ex-girlfriends, flirts outrageously with the waitresses, and ogles every *mujer* (woman) who walks by. No wonder this loser insisted on the *terraza* (terrace) even though it's cold outside. Then, just when you think you can sneak away, he orders two liquor anís and makes a romantic toast. You really have no interest in finding out how this *telenovela* (soap opera) ends.

What to do:

Drink both liquors, bang them down on the table cowboy-style, stand up, and be on your way. You don't owe him any kind of explanation, but if you want to say something to put a nail in the coffin on this sham of a date:

What to say:

TIENES MÁS MAGNETISMO QUE UN BOCATA DE IMANES.

"You've got as much magnetism as a magnet sandwich."

Or, you if that insult is a bit too clever for this guy, just keep it simple and tell him exactly what he can do:

¡COME MIERDAS!

"Eat shit!"

Why it's okay to say it:

It was only a mercy date to get this guy off your back. He is seriously insecure and in major need of a reality check. Plus a guy this challenged at the art of seduction is an insult to national pride where the idea of the suave Latin lover is still alive and well.

In the know:

There is some truth to the mach-ismo stereotype. Men in the land of Don Juan do tend to be quite forward with their attraction. Staring is permissible, as is cutting in on the dance floor. Also be fore-warned that the Spanish are much less squeamish about PDA than we are. In fact, they're not squeamish at all. Be prepared for your gag reflex to be jump-started whenever romance is in the air.

EXTRA CREDIT

You can flirt in Spain pretty much the same way you do Stateside. Here's how to say it:

LIGAR ("flirt").

SITUATION #27: EL RASTRO RASCAL

It's a warm and sunny Sunday morning in Madrid, and you decide to spend it at El Rastro, the large open-air market. You'd been told to watch for pickpockets and that bargaining is encouraged, but you hadn't counted on being taken for some gullible tourist. You've just turned onto the Calle Ribera de Curtidores when you spot the perfect "boots of Spanish leather" at a colorful stand. You overhear the salesperson tell the woman before you that the boots are 150 euros. When you step up, however, he tells you that they're 200 euros. Even though you explain that you understand Spanish, and that you heard him give a lower price to someone else, he holds to the ludicrous sum.

What to do:

If you really want the boots, do your best to be really polite and bargain. Then when they're safely in your hands, leave him with something he won't forget.

What to say:

¡CAPULLO, VAS A TIMAR A TUS MUERTOS!

Literally: "Pr**ck, go and cheat your dead!"

In Spain, insulting someone's dead is incredibly offensive, so he'll understand your full meaning.

Why it's okay to say it:

Ever since Dylan's 1963 hit, all Americans have come to Spain in search of sun, great food, wine, and boots of Spanish leather...and you're not leaving without yours!

In the know:

Madrid's famous flea market takes place every Sunday and public holiday in the barrio de Embajadores. You'll find lots of unusual antiques, curiosities, and collectibles; it's a real experience just to enjoy the sights and smells and energy of the market.

EXTRA CREDIT

Money seems to inspire lots of slang in any language. In the U.S., we say bucks, greenbacks, smackeroos, dead presidents, dough, ducats, mullah...the list could go on. Some equivalents in the former land of the peseta:

PASTA

CUARTOS

PELAS

GUITA

SITUATION #28: NEVERMIND THE BOLLOCKS

You and your friend join a group of a British exchange students one night in Barrio Húmedo in León. Even though the town is known for its great little *pinchos* (tapas, served with a *pincho*, or "toothpick"), everyone seems a lot more interested in the *bebidas* (drinks), the *tía buenas* (hot women), and *el fútbol*, than in getting anything to eat. Finally, you convince the bunch to stay long enough to order up a bunch *banderillas* (another name for *tapas*), and the Brits go at the olives and anchovies with such vigor you can hardly get one in your mouth before the bowls are empty. On the next round, you try to eat faster, but when someone stabs you with a toothpick for the fifth time, you decide that enough is enough.

What to do:

Tell these thugs that, in case they hadn't noticed, the sun had indeed set on the British Empire. Next, ask them to please put the toothpicks down before someone gets hurt. When you're sure no one's packing wood, tell them:

What to say:

¡OS VOY A METER LOS PALILLOS POR EL CULO!

Literally: "I am going to stick the toothpicks up your ass!"

Culo is a slang word for "ass."

And if one more person dares to run you through with a tiny wooden weapon again, then stand up quietly, dump the banderillas onto the offender's lap in a dramatic motion, and yell:

¡VETE A FOLLAR!

"Go f**ck yourself!"

In the know:

Sometimes called the Pilar of Hércules, there is a limestone from the Jurassic period that sits at the end of Spain, the southernwest tip of Europe, and it's actually part of the British Empire. This monolith is the Rock of Gibraltar and was handed over to Great Britain in 1713 at the end of the Spanish War of Succession. The 30,000 inhabitants speak a mix of Spanish and English so if you go you'll be well-served by brushing up on insults in both languages.

EXTRA CREDIT

Here are Spanish translations of some great British zingers: "Cock up" (to screw up, a screw-up)

FOLLÓN

"Grotty" (dirty, dowdy)

MUGRIENTO

"Lager lout" (binge-drinking thug)

GAMBERRO BORRACHO

"Pillock" (idiot)

SITUATION #29: MIRA, MIRA ON THE WALL...

You're touring Park Güell with a group of mostly Spanish-speaking tourists. One guy elbows you and says *"Mira, mira"* ("Look, look") every time he sees something that catches his eye. You really just want to enjoy the wonderful, meandering park without his two *pesetas* every fifteen feet. The worst part is that this guy points out the most non-issue sightings—like a pigeon or a woman eating *churros*.

What to do:

Duck out of the way next time he elbows you. Pretend you're a matador and wait until the last second, then pull away so Elbow Guy loses his balance. You've got to stay vigilant so you can *olé* your way out of his grasp each time. If he doesn't get the hint (and he probably won't), yell this so the entire tour group can hear it:

What to say:

¡NO ME TOQUES LOS COJONES!

Literally: "Don't touch my balls!"

Basically: "Don't bother me!"

Just because women don't have literal balls doesn't mean they can't curse like they do; both men and women in Spain commonly use this expression.

Why it's okay to say it:

Your mother lied to you. Just because you don't have anything nice to say DOESN'T mean you shouldn't say anything at all.

In the know:

Gaudí's intention was to build a garden suburb overlooking the center of Barcelona. In the end, only two houses were built, but the architect's whimsical designs and undulating shapes have become part of the landscape, creating the magical park several million visitors enjoy each year.

SITUATION #30: REAL HOMBRES EAT MEAT

You're at Celler Sa Premsa in Palma, and you explain to the waiter in very clear Spanish that you don't eat meat. You're used to the unfriendly attention and dumb jokes associated with being a veggie ("*Hey Paco, we've got a carrot-killer!*"). You can handle the jokes, but what annoys you the most is that the waiter keeps suggesting inappropriate dishes for you to order— *jamón* (ham), *chorizo* (blood sausage), or partridge. Just when you think he's getting tired, he moves onto seafood.

What to do:

Never forget you're in a land where bull-fighting isn't just considered a sport but an art form. Ask for a *paella* with only vegetables. And tell the guy where he can stick his *jamón*.

What to say:

MÉTETE EL JAMÓN POR EL CULO.

"Stick the ham up your ass."

Why it's okay to say it:

It's true, a decade or so ago you could have walked in on stilts and attracted less attention, but in any major city in Western Europe, being a vegetarian is NOT a newsworthy event.

In the know:

If you want to stick to tofu-friendly joints, it would be a big mistake to visit Museo del Jamón, where pig legs are splayed out, hanging from the ceiling. Even in restaurants with less gratuitous décor, however, be forewarned that this is a country where vegetarians are often served ham. It's not done maliciously: many Spaniards simply don't consider ham meat. Americans aren't the only ones who believe you can't be a real man if you don't eat meat.

EXTRA CREDIT

When it comes to animal-inspired insults, some of these cross language barriers. Cow, pig, donkey, and dog (bitch) are all pretty much used to the same effect in Spanish as in English to mean fat, dirty, dumb, and mean.

BURRO/BURRA ("donkey")

CABRÓN/CABRONA ("goat")

FOCA ("seal" used to mean fat)

VACA ("cow" used to mean fat)

HIJO/HIJA DE PERRA ("son/daughter of a bitch")

CERDO/CERDA ("pig")

SITUATION #31: GETTING SOAKED WITHOUT A DROP TO DRINK

You're in a trendy tapas bar in Ciutat Vella, but you have a long night planned and don't want to blow your wad in one spot. Unfortunately the waiter is giving you a hard time. You order *agua del grifo* (tap water), and he claims they don't have a tap; you ask for *cañas* (house beers), and he says they just ran out; and when you inquire about the wine, he directs you to the most expensive *botella* (bottle).

What to do:

If you're up for a gamble, point to a nearby table where the guests don't look like royalty, and say you'll have what they're having. You could also conjure up *Five Easy Pieces* with this sarcastic request: ask the waiter to prepare some rice; tell him not to put the rice in the pot, not to heat the water, but pour the water into a glass and bring it out:

Prepare un arroz, pero no ponga el arroz en el cazo y no caliente el agua. Entonces ponga el agua en un vaso y me lo sirve.

If you think your clever joke will be lost on the arrogant *gilipollas* (pr**ck), then maybe it's time to move on to the next venue for the evening. But before you go, give your sniffy server a piece of your mind...

What to say:

ESTO HASTA EL MOÑO CABRÓN, ME LARGO.

Literally: "I have had it up to here, you pr**ck, I'm off."

Why it's okay to say it:

This guy may think you're one taco short of a combo plate, but he's got another thing coming.

In the know:

It's rare to be charged for tap water in Spain although it does happen. In that case restaurants are required to include it on the menu with a price. Speaking of service, in general, don't take offense if you don't get the kind of attention you're used to stateside. Spanish waiters and waitresses tend to be a bit more mechanical and distant, attending to a great many tables and not getting personally involved with customers. That being said, you might actually find it a relief to not know the name, hometown, and astrological sign of your server!

EXTRA CREDIT

In Spain, if someone "just fell off a turnip truck" or isn't "playing with a full deck," you would say:

SER MÁS CORTO QUE LAS MANGAS DE UN CHALECO

Literally: "To be shorter than the sleeves of a vest." *Corto* is slang for "thick."

LO ÚNICO QUE TIENE EN LA CABEZA ES EL PELO.

Literally: "The only thing on their heads is hair." In Spanish, the word *en* means "in" and "on."

SITUATION #32: RADIO DAZE

As you're leaving the church at your friend's destination wedding in romantic Toledo, you run into a wannabe diva you've met several times before. She introduces herself to you with no sign of recognition. Later you smile at her on the dance floor; no reaction. When you catch up to the *mujer* at the bar and explain that you've met her several times in the past as well as earlier that day, she claims not to recognize you — she's far too busy with her burgeoning career to remember the face of every person she meets.

What to do:

When you see what kind of drink she orders, shake your head with a knowing look. When she gives you a puzzled expression, tell her seeing the drink reminded you that she'd had about ten of those the last time you saw each other; that's probably why she's blacking out. She tells you no, that you must be mixing her up with someone else; you probably just recognize her voice because of several recent voiceovers and radio spots:

What to say:

TIENES UNA CARA IDEAL PARA TRABAJAR EN LA RADIO.

"Well, you've certainly got a face that was made for radio."

Why it's okay to say it:

This *creída* (woman who is full of herself) was absolutely asking for it. Maybe she'll think twice before setting herself up so easily next time.

In the know:

At Spanish weddings, the fireworks aren't only metaphorical. While the crowds are throwing petals or roses on the happy couple, you'll often be treated to a display of *petardos* (fireworks) going off in the background.

EXTRA CREDIT

When you're not feeling particularly inventive with your insults, you could always just say:

LO MISMO TE DIGO

("back at you")

SITUATION #33: GOT AGUA?

You're stuck in a tour group at the World Heritage Sight of Segovia with a Hispanic version of the Brady Bunch, but you've luckily been able to ignore them for the first half of the trip, keeping your sights on the illustrious *alcázar* (castle). As soon as you break out your water, however, the kids are all over you like sand in a bathing suit. You give them each a sip, but then you want your water back. The mother, meanwhile, keeps worrying that the kids are getting dehydrated and repeatedly gives you a series of pleading looks.

What to do:

First, finish the water. There's no sense in everyone getting heatstroke. Next, when you get to the Roman aqueducts, tell the kids to pay attention: even in the second century b.c. people knew enough to plan ahead so they'd have water to drink.

What to say:

MIRA QUE NO TRAER AGUA, SOIS MAS CORTOS QUE EL RABO DE UN CONEJO.

"I can't believe you didn't bring water, you are shorter than a rabbit's tale."

Corto means "short," but here it is slang for "thick."

Why it's okay to say it:

You came prepared, it's not your fault these little entitled *mocosos* (brats) have never heard
of Sigg bottles. You probably shouldn't have given them a sip in the first place; maybe you're hearing too much about medieval torture on the castle tour, but you can't help

In the know:

Today there are approximately 2500 castles in Spain; it is believed that there were once four times that many. Like many Spanish castles, the uniquely-shaped Alcázar of Segovia (it looks like the bow of a ship) was originally an Arab fortification.

SITUATION #34: EMPIRE STRIKES BACK

It's true your Yoda backpack is a bit childish, but it was the only one left in Target, and you grabbed it on your way to the airport. You'd been warned to be on the lookout for pickpockets and muggers, but a birthday party brigade mistaking your backpack for a *piñata*? You never saw that one coming. Just as you step into one of the courtyards of the Alhambra Palace, you feel a smack and turn around to see a whole *pandilla* (gang) of spoiled brats chasing after you calling for *azúcar* (sugar) and shouting "Off with his head!"

What to do:

Of course take off the backpack and hope that Yoda's force is enough to fend off the candy-hungry hoard.

What to say:

OS VOY A PARTIR LA CARA A HOSTIAS!

"I'm going to kick your face!"

This is an insult because of the religious reference incorporated in the phrase (*hostia* meaning "host").

Why it's okay to say it:

It's just self-defense, and besides, isn't the person hitting you at least supposed to be blindfolded?

In the know:

There's a traditional song that kids sing when striking at the piñata that begins:

> *Dale, dale, dale,*
> *no pierdas el tino;*
> *Porque si lo pierdes*
> *pierdes el camino.*

"Hit it, hit it, hit it (or 'go, go, go')
Don't lose your aim
Because if you lose it (your aim)
You will lose the path."

In another context, it actually makes a pretty good self-help mantra.

SITUATION #35: CHILI RECEPTION

You knew it was a mistake to keep nodding as the waiter poured *pimientos* (peppers) onto your tortilla. Now everyone in the restaurant is staring as your eyes tear up, your face goes as red as a matador's cape, and you begin gulping down gallons of water at an alarming rate. But you can't believe it...while you're gasping for air, the locals are laughing at your misery!

What to do:
Bribe the waiter to switch a plate of regular *pimientos* with the ultra-spicy and unpredictable *pimientos de Padrón* and give it to the ringleader of the peanut gallery, compliments of the chef. On your way out, stop by your target who'll be gasping for air himself by that time and say:

What to say:

ASÍ TE AHOGES, CABRÓN.

"I hope you choke, you pr**ck."

Why it's okay to say it:
You're letting this guy off easy. If he dares answer back, there's a giant bag of salt you'd be happy to pour on him.

In the know:

The idea that Spaniards love spicy food is another example of Mexican traditions incorrectly getting associated with Spain (think Mariachi and tacos). In truth, many Spaniards are happy to add a shake or two of paprika for spice, not much more. However, a *variety* of spices is extremely important to national cuisine: remember what Columbus was looking for when he stumbled upon America?

EXTRA CREDIT

We use the term **"spicy"** to mean risqué. In Spanish, you might say:

ARRIESGADO ("risqué")

SUBIDO DE TONO

This literally translates to "with the volume pumped up," but the implied meaning is risqué.

SITUATION #36: THERE GOES THE SUN

You're at the Caleta beach in Cádiz and have just finished covering yourself with coconut oil so you can work on your tan. The beach is hot, the top-less ladies are hotter, and you couldn't be happier. You've just sprawled out face down on your towel to soak up the rays when some jackasses with fake tans the color of saffron seasoning set up giant umbrellas, blocking all your sun.

What to do:

Ask them politely to move their umbrella. If they refuse, shake your towel out so the sand blows in their direction. Before you move on to a new locale, throw this insult in their direction:

What to say:

SOIS UN VERDADERO COÑAZO.

Literally: "You are a real c**nt."

Basically: "You are a pain in the neck."

Why it's okay to say it:

This is *el país del sol* (country of the sun). If it were *el país* of anything else, maybe you wouldn't have reacted so strongly.

In the know:

Cádiz is the oldest city in Western Europe. In Ancient Greek myth, Hercules founded the city after killing a multi-headed beast...maybe not unlike the one giving you your own private solar eclipse.

EXTRA CREDIT

You'll likely run into a lot of unwelcome people just as soon as you find the perfect spot...whether it's at the beach, a café, or a movie theater. Several ways to say persona non grata in Spanish are:

GENTUZA ("riffraff")

CHUSMA ("mob")

MORRALLA ("rabble")

SITUATION #37: LOCO FLAMENCO

You've never loved the eerie tremolos of flamenco guitar, but you've been positively scarred by a guy sharing your room at a hostel in Benicarlo. Those *tientos* and *tangos* make terrible lullabies – the jarring lack of tempo is enough to give you arrhythmia, and the discordant chords sound like the backdrop to one of Buñuel's nightmare scenes.

What to do:
Make a mix of the greatest riffs by Slash, Van Halen and the Edge; when you hit the sheets, turn those bad boys up to ten.

What to say:

TE VOY A DEJAR MÁS SORDO QUE UNA TAPIA

Literally: "I'm going to make you as deaf as a wall."

In the know:
Most of Spain's 140 youth hostels (*albergues de juventud*) have an 11pm curfew which means you'll have barely started dinner by the time you need to check in. Don't confuse these hostels with *hostales*, the equivalent of our economy hotels.

EXTRA CREDIT

In this case, all you're after is a few effective ways to say SHUT UP:

CIERRA EL PICO

This literally translates to "shut your beak," and isn't considered very rude.

CÁLLATE LA PUTA BOCA

"Shut your f**cking mouth." Um, this is obviously a lot worse.

SITUATION #38: AN EXCRUCIATING EPIPHANY

On holiday in Majorca, you become friendly with a family staying in your villa. One evening after dinner they invite you to an Epiphany party taking place the next day (January 6). You bring fresh flowers and a box of *churros*, and you're excited to finally the try the *pescado* (fish) in Spain. Everything is going along well until the host swoops in with a beautiful 12th Night Bread. You all dig in, and two bites later you've nearly broken a tooth on something harder than last year's *turrón* (nougat treat served at Christmas). You excuse yourself to the restroom, but the group comes after you like a lynch mob, demanding the coin that was buried in the cake and implying that you've ruined the whole point of *La Fiesta de los Tres Reyes Magos* (The Feast of the Three Kings).

What to do:
Spit out the coin. Make sure your molars are all intact and, when the kids are out of earshot, tell the couple:

What to say:

¡ME CAGO EN LA HOSTIA, CASI ME JODO UNA MUELA!

"Holy shit, I almost got one of my teeth f**cked!"

Why it's okay to say it:
You made it clear that you'd never heard of celebrating the Epiphany. How were you supposed to know that the *pièce de résistance* of the celebration was a dirty piece of copper? Forget the manifestation of the Christ Child; they're lucky there's no manifestation of a lawsuit.

In the know:
In Spain, children leave out polished shoes on the night of January 6 for gifts from the wise men, similar to the American tradition of leaving stockings out on Christmas Eve. A drink and a snack are often left out for the King, along with water for the camels.

SITUATION #39: FROST IN TRANSLATION

You're on a foreign exchange program in Madrid, and your host mother encouraged you to sign up for an *intercambio* — an hour meeting between an English speaker and a Spanish speaker where you trade off languages, to each other's benefit. It seemed like a good way to get your feet wet with the language, without jumping into a baptism by fire. Your partner did a great job translating some of Cervantes' poetry. You were a little less ambitious, choosing the New England poet Robert Frost. You're really enjoying the exercise until you realize this *capullo* (d**ck) is cringing every time you mispronounce a word. You feel like you're on *American Idol*, and the judges are making no effort to conceal their disdain.

What to do:
Don't be intimidated. Keep reading until you finish the poem – even if you've got miles to go. When you're done, tell the *criticón* (faultfinder):

What to say:

MÉTETE LA LENGUA EN EL CULO.

Literally: "Stick your tongue up your ass."

Basically: "Shut the f**ck up."

Why it's okay to say it:

The whole point of the *intercambio* is to have an informal, relaxing way to improve your language skills simultaneously. It should be a symbiotic relationship, but if this pretentious *gilipollas* (pr**ck) is going to make a face every time you don't sound like you're in an Almodóvar movie, you might as well leave.

In the know:

Miguel de Cervantes Saavedra is Spain's national poet, though he's best known for his fiction; *Don Quixote* is considered by many to be the first modern novel.

SITUATION #40: HIT THE ROAD, JACINTO!

In a weak moment during your semester abroad you let your charming history professor set you up with her nephew, figuring it'd be a good way to meet other students. You *quedais a tomar algo* (arrange to go for a drink/go out), and it went okay. He mostly talked about himself, but you were willing to attribute that to nerves. Somehow after lots of *vino* (wine), you ended up back at your apartment. You're definitely not crazy about him, but let's face it — you won't be doing much talking. You're about to dim the lights, when the *sobrino* (nephew) kicks off his shoes in the middle of the living room, pours himself a drink, opens a jar of olives, and flops down in front of the TV.

What to do:
Turn the TV off, hand him his shoes, and let him know the whole *mi casa, tu casa* thing isn't working.

What to say:

ANDA, COMPRATE UN BOSQUE Y PIERDETE!

Literally: "Come on, buy a forest and get lost in it!"
Basically: "Get the f**ck out of here!"

Why it's okay to say it:
It was nice of you to invite him up, and you do appreciate him not putting the slimy moves on immediately, but when a jar of olives is more appealing to him than your plunging neckline, it's time to say *adios*!

EXTRA CREDIT

Let's say you really were interested in a little after-dinner action. How would you say it so Jacinto would be sure to understand?

¿FOLLAMOS?

"Shall we f**ck?"

SITUATION #41: THE BAREFOOT CONTESSA

It's a Saturday night in Barcelona and you're dressed to the nines or, as the Spanish say, *de punta en blanco*. You even managed to sneak in a pedicure, so you choose strappy sandals to show off your pretty pink toenails. After a great *tapas* stroll and a few cocktails at Rita Blue, you head to the nightclubs, but you're shocked that at the waterfront Salsa Club they stop you at the door for violating dress code. You give the bouncer an outraged look, but he points to your shoes and says no one can get in with flip-flops.

What to do:

Bend down, take off one of the sandals, hold it up to the bouncer's face and say "Do these look like flip-flops to you?" He'll likely give you a "Do I look like I care?" expression, at which point you can put the non-flip flop back on, flip the bird, and say...

What to say:

¡QUÉ TE FOLLE UN PEZ ESPADA!

Literally: "Go and get f**cked by a swordfish."

Basically: "Go f**ck yourself."

Why it's okay to say it:

You put a lot of effort into your outfit. Dress codes are to keep everyone looking up to snuff, and you've seen about ten fashion DON'TS slip in already.

In the know:

Catalans are fond of designer clothes. Do pay attention to style, but don't dress too provocatively; mini-skirts and scanty-halter tops will bring disapproving looks. And of course avoid shorts unless you wanted to be pegged for an American faster than you can say "Superbowl Sunday."

SITUATION #42: SEA DREAMS

You're spending a month in Valencia so you decide to answer a classified ad in *Levante*, the city's daily paper, for a beautiful, spacious one-bedroom with a dryer and a view of the water. What you find when you get there is a tiny, dank little *estudio* with a window to an alley shaft and a clothesline. You demand to know where the view of the water is, and the landlord shows you the bathtub, pointing out that there's no door, which gives you a straight shot of *el baño* (the bathroom) from anywhere you stand in the main room.

What to do:

Say *¡Venga, hombre!* (Yeah right, you've got to be kidding!) to this guy and, if you have the energy, prop yourself up outside the apartment and let any prospective renters know that Spain's lemon shortage is over.

What to say:

ESTATE AL LORO QUE TE VAN A DAR GATO POR LIEBRE.

Literally: "Be at the parrot, they are going to give you a hare instead of a rabbit."

Basically: "Be on the ball, they are going to rip you off."

"Be at the parrot" is slang for "Be on the ball."

Why it's okay to say it:

Talk about *caveat emptor*!

In the know:

If you're in Spain for Holy Week (the week before Easter), don't miss Valencia's festival; even if you've been duped a few times, the parades, fireworks, and parties of *Semana Santa* may just make you a believer.

EXTRA CREDIT

Wondering how to say con-artist/scammer/cheat in Spanish? There are a surprising number of choices:

TIMADOR ("swindler")

LADRÓN ("thief")

ESTAFADOR ("swindler", "fraudster")

EMBAUCADOR ("trickster")

TRILERO ("card sharp")

SITUATION #43: MATADOR BRATS

You have no interest in attending a bullfight, even though locals in Ciudad de Rodrigo keep asking if you plan to go. On the morning of the *fiesta brava* you decide to go for a quiet stroll when you see some beautiful fabrics in a store window. Once inside you pick out a lovely scarf. Just as you get back out and start to take your new scarf out of the bag, three kids grab it and begin swinging it around like a cape, acting out a bullfight.

What to do:
It's imperative that you harness the element of surprise here: charge the offenders head down, grab the *mantilla* (shawl), and shout:

What to say:

SOIS MÁS SIMPLES QUE EL MECANISMO DE UN CHUPETE.

> Literally: "You are as simple (thick) as the mechanism/workings of a pacifier."
>
> Basically: "You are a bunch of idiots."

Why it's okay to say it:
You were peacefully minding your own business, keeping your disdain for the bullfighting tradition to yourself. The kids wanted to create a spectacle, and caught you off guard. Besides, no one touches your brand new pashmina unless they want to rumble. "You want a fight, *picadores*? I'll give you a fight."

In the know:

Much to the horror of many Americans, bullfighting is still popular in Spain and other parts of the Latin world, perhaps chronicled most famously in Hemingway's *Death in the Afternoon*.

SITUATION #44: THE ARTFUL DODGER

You're at a small art gallery in Gran Canaria checking out the work of a local artist. Thank *Dios* you managed to score a few glasses of *cava* before getting trapped by an art history professor draped in a colorful shawl and, by the looks of it (you're trying to keep your eyes focused on the horizon), almost nothing else. She has you cornered by a rather lewd sculpture and has been dissecting the minutiae of how Goya's *Nude Maja* differs from his *Clothed Maja* for the past twenty minutes. You're missing out on the rest of the paintings, you're bored to tears and, quite frankly, things are starting to feel a little awkward.

What to do:

Start sliding toward the floor, citing an overdose of surrealism. If that doesn't work, then it's time to inject some much-needed reality into this kook's life:

What to say:

ERES MÁS ABURRIDA QUE UN MOSQUITO LOBOTOMIZADO.

"You are more boring than a lobotomized mosquito."

Why it's okay to say it:

You'd need to wash your mouth out with a lot more than soap if this woman had her way with you.

In the know:

Be thankful this *excéntrica* (eccentric) launched right into the modern art period. If she'd started at the beginning, she'd have to go back 32,000 years to Spain's prehistoric cave paintings. You'd hate to see where she'd take a conversation about the ancient Iberian bull statues of Avila!

EXTRA CREDIT

Let's face it, you'll be ill-prepared in any country if you don't know at least half a dozen vulgar ways to refer to the centerpiece of the male anatomy. Here are a few to get you started:

PICHA

CIPOTE

POLLA

NABO

SITUATION #45: FRESH FRUIT

You're at a *frutería* getting a big order for your friend's fiesta, and the pushy crowd feels more like a mosh pit. An angry looking teenage boy, surely sent to do errands, asks *"Quién es el ultimo?"* ("Who is last in the line?"), and then proceeds to stand next to you rather than behind you. Every time you move, he's right up there next to you. Honestly, you did enough maraca-shaking last night, and you don't feel like putting the effort into shaking him off now.

What to do:

Let him get ahead of you. People like this are often in it for the struggle. When you fold, you win. Making a grand display of letting him go first will also probably humiliate him more than the quiet battle to the register. Still, if he doesn't look embarrassed enough, don't let him off the hook entirely.

What to say:

HAY DÍAS TONTOS Y TONTOS TODOS LOS DÍAS.

Literally: "There are stupid days and stupid (people) every day."

Basically: "You are dumber than dumb."

Why it's okay to say it:

The Spanish don't "line up" like we do, but they do respect order, asking "Who's the last one?" and respectfully staying behind that person.

In the know:

Be careful around the Spanish and their produce. Maybe you've heard of *La Tomatina* in Buñol. The highlight of their yearly end of summer festival is a massive food fight where participants throw roughly 100,000 tomatoes at each other.

EXTRA CREDIT

Wondering what the Spanish equivalent of our fruit-inspired insults are?

She's bananas (crazy): *ESTÁ COMO UNA CABRA* — "She's a goat."

She's a bad apple: *MANZANA PODRIDA* — "She's a bad apple."

Sour grapes: *ENVIDIA* — "Envy"

5 WAYS TO GET SLAPPED BY A WOMAN

ERES UN PEDAZO GOLFA.
"You are a whore."

VAYA PAR DE TETAS
"What a pair of tits."

PENDÓN DESOREJADO
Literally: "Whore without ears"
Basically: "Whore"

MÁS PUTA QUE LAS GALLINAS.
"You are more promiscuous than a hen."

ZORRA
"Vixen", used to mean "whore"

5 WAYS TO INSULT A GUY'S MANHOOD

MARICÓN
"Homosexual"

CABRÓN
"Cuckold"

CORNUDO Y APALEADO
"A cuckold and beaten up"

CHULO PUTAS
"Pimp"

PICHACORTA
"Small penis"

5 INSULTS THAT COULD GET YOU LYNCHED

ME CAGO EN TUS MUERTOS.
"I shit on your dead."

ME CAGO EN LA LECHE QUE TE DIERON A MAMAR.
"I shit on the milk you sucked as a baby."

MAMÓN
Literally "sucker," but this is a really rude and offensive insult in Spain.
It implies the person is a homosexual.

GILIPOLLAS
"Pr**ck"

CHÚPAME LA POLLA.
"Suck my d**ck."

5 OF THE BEST "YOUR MOTHER" INSULTS

HIJO DE PUTA
"Son of a whore"

ME CAGO EN TU MADRE.
"I shit on your mother."

PUTA LA MADRE, PUTA LA HIJA, PUTA LA MADRE QUE LAS PARIÓ.
Literally: "Whore the mother, whore the daughter, whore the mother
who gave birth to them."

JODE A TU MADRE.
"F**ck your mom."

LA MADRE QUE TE PARIÓ
Literally: "The mother who gave you birth"
Basically: This is used to mean "f**ck you."